soft thorns

soft thorns

bridgett devoue

Andrews McMeel
PUBLISHING®

chapters

my letter to you

through this past year my book has been out, i've been asked the same questions time and time again, but one always stands out to me: *why did you write Soft Thorns?* and my reply is always the same: *it wasn't my choice.* this book has been burning a hole into my heart for months, maybe even years before it was ever published. when you know something is the right time, you truly feel it, deep inside a part of your soul that the world cannot get to. this is where your truth lies, and mine was pleading with me to share its message with the world.

i was going through a difficult time in my life, with the odds seemingly stacked against me. i had developed chronic pain that no doctors could diagnose, putting my work life and hopes of achieving my dreams on hold, all while experiencing my first real breakup. to cope with these feelings, with pen in hand, i began a therapeutic dance, releasing my pain onto pieces of paper. and without any thought or intention, tiny poems began to appear. i've always been drawn to short yet powerful poetry. i would write pages and pages of prose but always found myself taking out words and condensing the emotion into its most impactful form.

using my pen as a north star of sorts, i was able to guide myself out of a deep depression. i finally got life-changing treatment for my pain, i was passionate and ready to chase after my dreams again, and my heart had healed into a stronger version of itself. i looked in the mirror one day and almost didn't recognize the strong and confident woman staring back . . . and then it all hit me: i had all these painful, scary, and depressing days to thank for the person i had become. if i hadn't hit my proverbial rock bottom, i would not have been able to plant my roots and grow upward.

this knowledge, that even our most discouraging moments are where we learn and grow the most (therefore we should not fear them but embrace them) begged to be shared. but i didn't want to simply repeat these words verbatim. . . . no. i wanted people to live this truth as i had . . .

and here is where all those tiny poems scribbled on paper came into play. as i read through notebook after notebook, page after page, i felt my stitched-up heart coming undone at the seams and a flood of emotions washing over me. as i continued to read, moving through the poems of pain into lessons of forgiveness, my heart grew, as threads of understanding and hope wove themselves into it. by the end, my heart was, yet again, even stronger than it had already been. and it was here that *Soft Thorns* was born.

it's been an incredible journey, releasing a piece of my soul out into the world, and getting to connect with my readers over beautiful stories of how my words touched their hearts. but the truth is, their words have touched my soul just as strongly. because the story doesn't just end with me publishing a book. using social media as a platform to speak to my readers every day, *Soft Thorns* has become a living, breathing piece of me that is also a piece of everyone who has ever read it. we are all connected by the human vulnerabilities shared in this book, and therefore none of us are ever alone in our feelings, because there is always someone out there feeling the exact same thing. if you ever have something burning a hole into your heart, please listen to it. trust it to guide you to your destiny. take my journey as an example that you can achieve anything your heart desires, as long as you simply listen to it.

- bridgett devoue

i've been called brave
for my writing
but that label does not
belong to me

you are the brave one

without your open heart
my words are nothing
but meaningless groups
of letters on paper

you give them meaning

you make me brave
and i'll forever
be grateful for that

bleed

i was born
with wide eyes
and a fragile heart
that never learned
to say *no*

i feel everything so deeply
like stones in my pockets
holding me under
to drown

as women
everyone thinks we're fine
because makeup hides
the sleepless nights
and the tears we cry

sweetheart
honey
babygirl
cutie

these are not my name
and i am not yours

but you use intimate words
to give yourself a false sense
of dominance over me

these are bullets you keep ready
for when you feel threatened
by my feminine energy

and they hurt like gunshots
so don't tell me
it's a good thing

you opened my door
without knocking first
and never asked
if i wanted a guest

anorexia is a jealous lover
who controls every part
of your life

she'll start speaking for you
and oh
how she loves to lie
(i'm fine is her favorite)

she doesn't want you
to be in love with another
so she'll plant seeds of doubt
in the minds of others
until eventually
even your own body
will turn on you

this is why no one loves you
your limbs will say
when you look in the mirror
until eventually
you stop looking

alone and blind
you stumble into
the arms of anorexia

an abusive lover
but the only one left

the more weight i lost
the more i shrank into myself
and out of the world's reach

i'm safer here
i told myself
starving to death

beauty is a curse
the rose knows well

always picked first
yet never a chance
to grow

beauty does not solve problems

it's just a different map
down the same road

someone once told me
they were scared of
the truth in my eyes

so i learned to live
my life blind

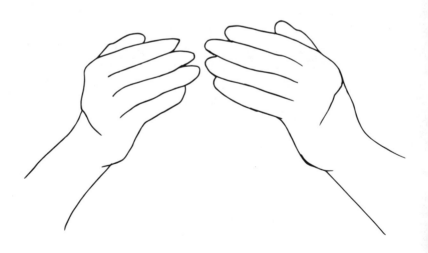

maybe we fall
in love with sad eyes
because we see our souls
reflected in them

i don't remember love as a child
my only teacher being magazines
and movie screens

so i spent my life
searching for fantasies

but a fantasy in real life
is also known as a lie

you can tear someone apart
just as easily with
unwanted names
an undressing gaze
perverted hands
a penetrating tongue

those scenes
will be replayed
and paused
rewound
and started again
with every touch
and lingering stare

penetration is not
the only rape

i met him at a bar when he told me
i don't date women under 5 foot 10

and i grew smaller
thinking i would never be
good enough for him

so when he invited me
back to his place for
drinks and some blow

i said yes
eager to prove
i was good enough

he got on his knees
and told me
you taste like cinnamon
and he didn't like
someone so fiery
so he used his finger
to put out my flame

it hurt
it always hurt
because my wax
would never
drip for him

at a party
where i shouldn't be
my best friend's brother
two years older than me
took my hand

we started dancing

the alcohol made me blush
and so did his touch
but my innocence
was showing
so i left him to sleep off
what was blinding me

but i woke to fingers like knives
ripping apart my insides

with each thrust
he carved out
more and more
of my soul
until i was nothing
but a pile of
meat and bones
lying on the floor

forever silent in shock
of what a friend
had just done

when you've been abused for so long
rape just feels like the next chapter
in a predictable novel

i woke up in a naked body
that was not my own
it felt foreign
numb

until i rolled over
and saw another
foreign body
rubber on the floor
a pill bottle
on the dresser
more intoxicating
than liquor
and red stains
on the sheets
where i had
apparently been

the moment i was
saving myself for
was *stolen*
and i wasn't even
allowed to remember it

scars may fade
but they last forever.

love

i wish we lived in a world
where it was safe to keep
our hearts unlocked

i always scared
everyone away
i wanted too much
they'd say

because if they wanted
to come inside of me
then i needed to know
what was inside of them

but whenever
i was allowed in
i found a maze
of stone walls
and barbed wire
lost inside the soul
of the wrong one

hopeless romantic
they'd say
and hopeless
i was quickly
becoming

if you're not going
to swim deep with me
then get out of my waters

as a little girl
i didn't dream
of being a ballerina

i dreamt of
exploring the world
holding your hand

i knew who you were
not by the color of your hair
but by the way you would look at me
and i would fall into your depths

i kept this dream hidden
protected from the bombs
being thrown at my heart

my hope was
becoming too battered
and i knew it was time
to surrender

but then walking down the street
your eyes met mine

and i fell

i used to think
love wasn't for me
that i wasn't worthy

but all it took was one hello
to change *everything*

my heart becomes so light
when i'm around you

it floats out of my chest
and takes all my pain
and suffering with it

your love is like an exorcism

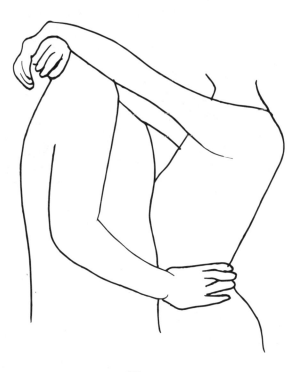

to see you happy
makes me happy
like our hearts
became one
the first time
we fell in love

because of you
i'm no longer hopeless
i'm just romantic

you're the one
who reminded me
i have a pulse

you call me a rose
because in your hands
i will always bloom

chemistry is the science
of making everyone else
but us disappear

we can't even do cute things
like watch movies or hold hands

our magnetism is so strong
we always end up as one

we know what the other needs
because it's what we need
in ourselves

bridgett devoue

there is an unspoken
truth between us

that both our hearts
weigh far too heavy
to keep up on their own

like a drug
i crave you
even though i know
you will destroy me

you're just standing there
watching me burn
wearing that crooked
smile of yours

a lighter in one hand
and my heart in the other

i think you like the show

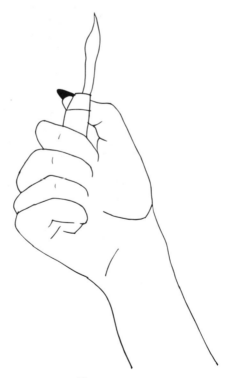

i know you're speaking
but i can't hear you
over the conversation
i'm having with your soul

you remind me
i used to be
fluent in love

let's keep the lights on
i trust you to still love me

i got undressed and he said
vulnerability looks good on you

i never knew a better sound
than my name on your lips

i know i'm not perfect
but i felt pretty damn close
when i was in your arms

in that moment
it was clear
that even though
we just met
i always knew
it was you

and i realize
no one has ever
really *touched* me
before you

so much more was
said in the unsaid

we never realize how
frozen we are until
someone starts to
melt our ice

i love your scars
they give my fingertips
a story to trace

making love with you
feels like a reunion

in another lifetime
we have definitely
done this before

i never thought
i would be a good mother
until you showed me
how endless
my love could be

i want to love you back together
to brush away the cobwebs
and show you the beauty
of your neglected soul

we have this *divine* bond

divine in the way that it's certainly
not from this lifetime

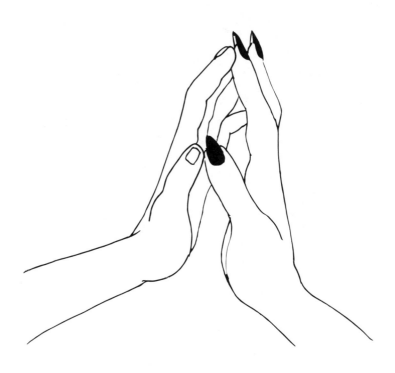

my soul craves a love
that's undeniably real

i want to experience
why we're here on earth

i can't help but think of forever
when i think of you

if it doesn't burn a little
then what's the point of
playing with fire?

scar

my baggage
you cannot carry

you can see the war
waging inside of me
you know how much
i want to tell you everything

to let the truth
spill from my lips
in a genuine display
of vulnerability

but even with
your caring eyes
and familiar soul
i'm scared because
i've never done this
before

you've already fallen
in love with my angels
so how could you ever
love my demons?

stop talking so much
i'm trying to cum

your thrusts become painful
as my oceans dry up
because there's nothing
more demeaning
than having no say
as to how your insides
are to be treated

just a body
just a hole

to you
i am nothing more
than some water
to swim in

we're lying in bed
after having sex

i know that look
when your eyes
turn distant
and drift upward

i can see you escaping
into the bed of another

the one you've been inside
the one still on your mind

and i finally accept
what we both already knew

i cannot satisfy you
in the only way
you will allow me to

you're having sex
while i'm making love

we crave intimacy
even when it hurts

i didn't tell you
because i trusted
you would sense
the pain in me

i believed we were so in tune
you would know instantly

but i was wrong

hearts break
when people change
but feelings stay
the same

you're saying
you're still here
like i'm an idiot
but i know very well
you left months ago

i felt you pack your bags
and walk out of my heart
and now i can't decide
what's worse

to live without you
or with a ghost of you

hell is watching something
that was your everything
slip away
and not being able
to do anything about it

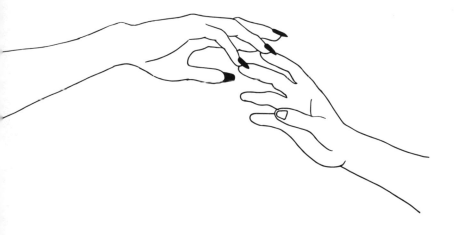

i can tell
when i'm with you
you're with her

you fell in love with my fire
so why are you trying
to put out my flame?

every time you text me
i turn into a little girl

blushing and butterflies

you let me experience
my lost childhood
and maybe this is why
your silence burns

why is it that
everyone can see
i'm suffering
but you?

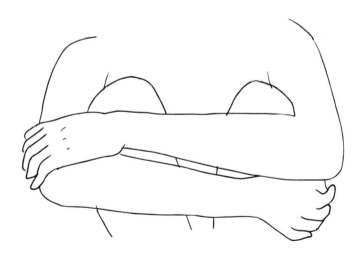

let's pretend like we're friends
(maybe then the feelings will disappear)

it's so painful to talk to you
because i just remember
everything you turned out
not to be

i don't want to date you
but i don't want you to be
in love with someone else

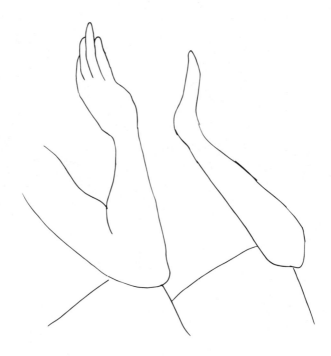

it's sad to think
we'll never make magic again

the world had no idea
what it was in for

i don't know how
to fall asleep anymore
without thoughts of you
holding me softly
while the rest
of the world crumbles
and only we remain steady

i stay up all night wondering
are you pretending to forget me too?

it's 4:30 a.m.
and i'm becoming weak
at the thought of being
in your arms again

i just want to know
do you dream of me too?

why am i more
naked and vulnerable
with your ghost
than i ever was
with you?

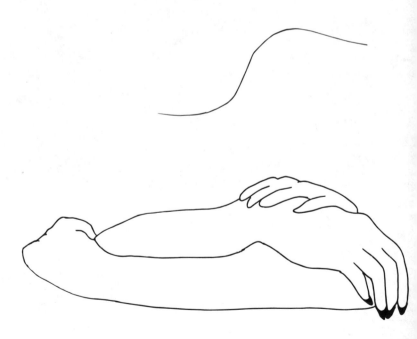

i can still close my eyes
and trace every curve
and dip of your soul

those who don't believe in ghosts
have never had a broken heart

your touch haunts
my daydreams

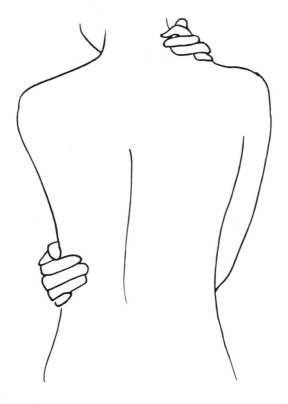

i wanted to show you my love
but you couldn't see me through
the walls around your heart

i knew i was playing
with fire when we met
so i couldn't blame you
when i got burned

i get into bed
and lay my head
on the pillow
facing you

god you're beautiful

i tell you how my day was
you laugh at a joke
our eyes meet
and i'm falling into
your depths again

i want to touch you

but i can't

i close my eyes
and turn over
but your ghost
comes closer
wrapping his arms
around my waist

he wipes the tears
from my eyes
telling me

forget him
you have me now instead

and it's like
you're breaking up with me
all over again

if i let go of you
i feel like i'm letting go
of a dream

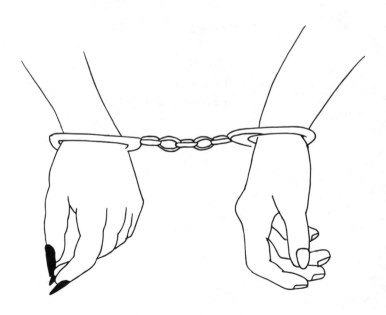

i know i should
but i'm not ready
to give up your memory

i gave you a home in my heart
and when you left
you forever took a
part of me with you

why do our hearts choose lovers
that make us suffer?

we used to say there was no way
we could ever not be in love

why did we jinx ourselves like that?

i'll forever live
in the palm
of your hand

and you
in the center
of my heart

i hold my breath
when i think of you
because each inhale
is a painful reminder
that i'm still living
without you

i'm not single
i'm haunted

i never told you
how much you hurt me
because even though you're gone
i'm still scared to lose you

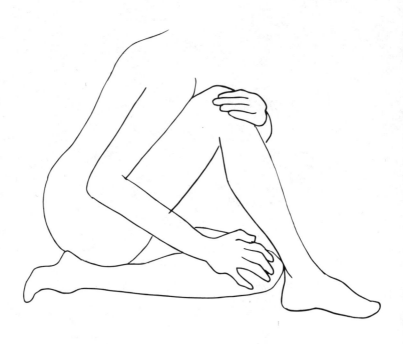

i haven't spoken to
anyone since you left

you stole all the words
from my heart

our souls fell in love
our egos broke us up

like a dying rose
starving for your sunlight
i'm wilting away

it's so painful seeing you
with your new girlfriend
because you're proud
to be with her

you take pictures together
you say *she's mine*

and it hurts to know
that in your eyes
i will always just be
a secret

being alone was never hard
before i met you

we used to lie in bed together
and trace stars into my ceiling

and now i have
a whole constellation
of broken dreams
above me

even in the arms
of a new lover
i'll still feel like
i'm cheating on you

i know we said goodbye
but i didn't know it was forever

i keep falling in love
with souls that feel
like yours

tonight
the stars are smiling
because of him

he makes me feel so at ease
walking around my walls
so lovingly

the moonlight reflecting
across his lips

*he's beautiful
but his smile . . .*

i'm trying to shake what i had seen
but my imagination is already
turning on me

. . . looks familiar

and the stars
begin to weep

i miss you

i thought i was free
when i escaped your prison

but love is a life sentence

i let you inside
my sacred corners
and now i'm worried
you'll never leave

you must think i'm crazy
for missing something
i never even had

to you
i may be many things
but i'll never be her

you were so gentle
when you were inside of me

how could you have been
so brutal with my heart?

i'm lonely
but i don't want company

i want to lie in bed alone
knowing someone else
is thinking of me

you walked away
far too easily
for me to believe
it was ever truly love

you begged to see all of me
so i showed you my heart

turns out
you just meant
my skin

you never loved me
you just wanted to
fuck me

and you were willing to say
whatever it took
to capture your prey

when you've been
fed lies for so long
you eventually lose
your appetite for love

when boys call me a heartbreaker
i tell them *i learned from the best*

your love was
everything to me

it changed my life
when you destroyed
the walls built up
around my heart

but i learned
people experience love
in different ways

and to you
i was just an escape

i have nothing left to say to you
because you're just a thief
who steals words
and disguises them
to fit your own needs

you'll never know all the ways
i died for you.

learn

goodbye is easy
everything after
is the hard part

i really wish
we could have been
everything i dreamed
we would be

but i forgot to ask
if you had the same
dreams as me

sometimes
we fall in love with ideas
not people

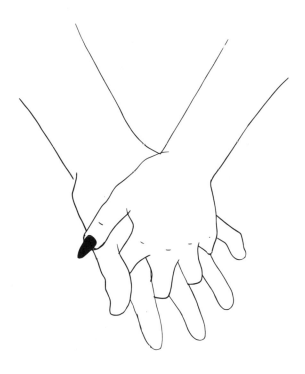

our most important conversations
were made in silence

your lack of words
has penetrated me
deeper than you ever did

i need to walk away
from the person you've become
because i've already said goodbye
to the one i fell in love with

bridgett devoue

this whole time
i've been loving
a memory

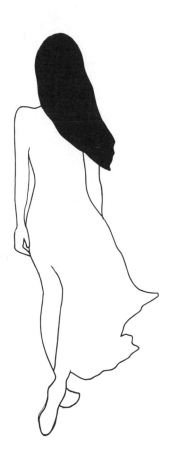

you killed me so many times
it's a miracle i'm still alive

eyes are the windows to the soul
they say

but to a narcissist
they're just another mirror

your words
dripped like honey
sticky
so they covered your lies
and made them
taste sweet

but of all the words
that left your lips
sorry
would have been
the sweetest

even though
you turned out to be a liar
within me grew a love
that was the most pure
and honest thing
i've ever known

bridgett devoue

love blossoms
no matter the soil

145

bittersweet defined us

bridgett devoue

nothing was ever easy
but maybe that was
the beauty of it

you left me
and i became
all the things
you said i wasn't
yet you will never
get to know it

you never have to
remind someone
to love you

you picked my petals
thinking i was a wallflower
not knowing i'm a rose
with thorns

that love i saw
reflected in your eyes
was not meant for me

it was meant for the world

i thought
i wasn't good enough
because you left me
but it's the opposite

*i have too much fire
and too much love*

you couldn't handle me
so you ran because
i am everything
you are not

your ghost may be gone
but i'm no longer lonely

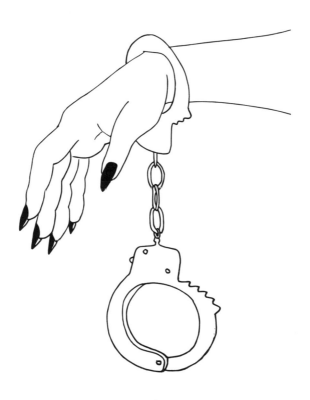

i'm angry
but i'm grateful
because even though
you tried to burn me
instead you just showed me
how to light my own flame

i lost love with you
but found love within me

never give up
because beautiful things
can be born from misery

don't be someone's "sometimes"

never judge a rose for her petals
she may still be blooming

in time
even the sharpest thorns
will become soft.

heal

bridgett devoue

love is a necessary tragedy

163

as women
we've grown deaf
to the whistles
and whispers
that come with
walking down the street

we've learned to keep
our heads down
growing small
into the shells
we never asked for

these habits leave scars
that will never heal
because we were born
into a world
where our bodies
do not belong
to us

these things happen to girls like you

this is a lie you have been told

he showed me a picture
of a beautiful girl
soft skin and lingerie

can you believe she's a lawyer?

words that crack like a whip
every time i hear them

can you believe?

yes
of course i can

i can believe a woman
who has long hair
big eyes
breasts and hips
and dripping curves
is capable
of studying in school
reading a book
writing a thesis
arguing a point
winning a case

appearance and intelligence
are not codependent
they coexist

your appearance
does not define
your intelligence

bridgett devoue

your appearance
is simply the cover
to your inner memoir

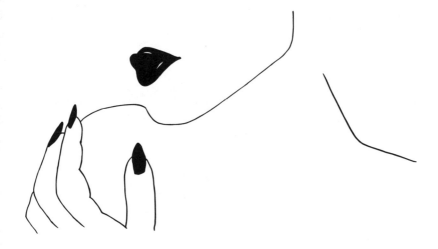

there are people
who don't want
you to heal
so they keep their
words sharp
to cut your heart
because they can't
suck the life
out of someone
who's not bleeding

remember
you are not their prey

do not get comfortable
in your story line

you have more power
than you know

only you can make
yourself a victim

there's healing power
in a simple apology
but when egos
get in the way
some would rather
hurt the ones they love
than admit they're
vulnerable

we're built to make mistakes
and also given the gift
to apologize

dear empath
sometimes it can be hard
to think and feel for yourself
because you were born
with the ability
to live in the thoughts
and hearts of others

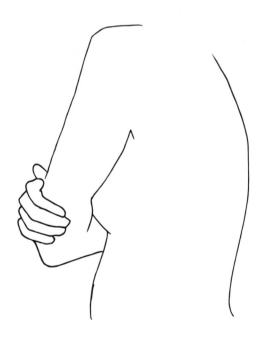

we choose to stay numb because
we think it keeps us safe

but the most dangerous thing
we can do is forget how to feel

when you've been
in pain for so long
not being in pain
becomes *painful*

when you get rid
of the source of your pain
that doesn't mean
you also get rid
of the habits
you used to cope

it may feel as if
getting rid of the pain
doesn't get rid
of anything at all

but this is where
you must trust time
starve out your old habits
and plant new ones
with love

demons try to control us
but out in the open
they're nothing more
than whispers
of a painful past

you will be safe in the right hands

love makes us immortal
in the heart of others
and mortal in our fear
that it could all be gone
one day

i thought he defined
what love should be
so i searched for
his hissing tongue
and venomous touch

until i realized i didn't want
another broken heart
or to be left
with the same mess
i had just cleaned up

so i found peace in
removing his definitions
from my vocabulary
but keeping him as a chapter
to reread in my diary

your past
is never truly
in the past

bridgett devoue

we're only haunted by the things
we refuse to accept

sometimes our hearts
flood with everything
being thrown at us
and acceptance is the raft
that will keep us afloat

it won't stop the storm
but we will not drown
so we can live to see
the sun come back out

you're going to suffer
you're going to feel
like your thoughts
have been hijacked
because all you can
think about is them

every time you're happy
you remember their smile
and every time you're sad
you remember why they're gone

your stomach will drop
every time your phone rings
and disappointment
will become a ritual
when you realize it's never them

there will be a fog
of uncertainty and doubt
everywhere you look
it will feel endless
because heartbreak
doesn't just disappear

but it fades

thank you for the scars
the right one will say
they're beautiful

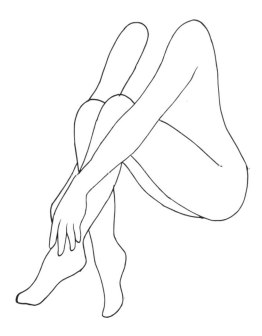

my heart is much
too big for my body
and maybe this is why
it always hurts

to anyone who has ever
filled your heart with sadness
and your eyes with tears
thank them

it's because of them
you're stronger and wiser
than you were then

we come into this world
like fresh clay
ready to be molded

our experiences shape
our opinions on everything
that comes after

*and this is where
belief systems are made*

not within the depths
of our hearts
but from the encounters
that bend and twist
our walls

people are not bad
people have simply lived

once i learned
that being pretty
was not a talent
i got my power back

we should always
search for depth
no matter how hard
beauty makes it
to look past
the surface

none of us are ever truly single

we all have a lifetime
of relationships that
live on in our hearts

you can't be feeling
the pain of a broken heart
if you didn't first experience
the beauty of love

sometimes
the most broken people
have the most love to give

own the strength
in your softness

you are always healing
so don't wait to start living

bridgett devoue

society teaches us to shrink
love teaches us to grow

please protect your inner romantic
because it's a beautiful thing
to prioritize love

romantics are the new rebels

when we were children
we had yet to be told
what society thinks

we only knew how to
listen to our hearts

we can't forget this
as we grow older
because our hearts
will tell us how to heal

the truth hurts because
we live in a world
so used to lies

we feel so alone
because there is a
whole universe
inside each of our minds
that we will never
get to experience
together

we're starving
for connection
not attention

that voice that tells you
you are not worthy
is not worthy
of your time

let oppression be the reason
you work harder than the rest

our darkest times
are when we learn
how deep we can swim
and where we get
the confidence
to never be fearful
of the water again

our experiences
are stored in our hearts
like a prized book collection

we must rewrite
the pages of our memories
so instead of hurt
these books teach us love

accept your heart will break
and trust that you will survive

don't let the one who broke your heart
help you build a new one

be grateful when someone
tears you apart

they just did the hard work for you

now you can start over and rebuild
with a stronger foundation

it's their loss
tastes bitter on my tongue
because it's not their loss

it's another's to gain

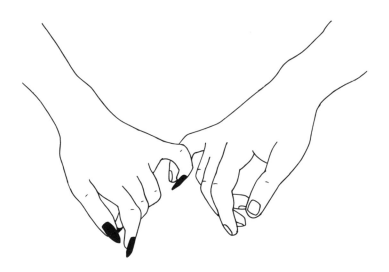

heartbreak is as life changing
as finding true love

broken hearts are beautiful
because they grow stronger each day

roses are proof that
you can protect yourself
while remaining soft

your weakest moments
are your strongest
in disguise

time will either
heal you or kill you

so if you're reading this
you are healing

i promise you

we are not born broken.

acknowledgments

To the ones who broke me
Thank you for lighting my flame; you inspired
me the most to succeed, because by breaking me
down, you gave me a chance at a clean start.

To my mom
The strongest woman I know.

To my dad
It took this long, but it all makes sense now.
Thank you.

To chloë frayne
Your heart is endless; thank you for showing me
what forever looks like.

And to you (yes, you)
This is my heart you're holding in your hands;
thank you for giving me a chance. I love you.

social media

Join Bridgett Devoue on the following:

- instagram.com/bridgettdevoue

- bridgettdevoue.tumblr.com

- twitter.com/bridgettdevoue

- pinterest.com/bridgett_devoue

- facebook.com/bridgettdevoue

Andrews McMeel Publishing
a division of Andrews McMeel Universal
1130 Walnut Street, Kansas City, Missouri 64106

www.andrewsmcmeel.com

19 20 21 22 23 BVG 10 9 8 7 6 5 4 3 2

ISBN: 978-1-4494-9688-3

Library of Congress Control Number: 2018942776

Editor: Patty Rice
Designer/Art Director: Spencer Williams
Production Editor: Elizabeth A. Garcia
Production Manager: Cliff Koehler